piano • vocal • guitar

AVRIL LAVIGNE
UNDER MY SKIN

ISBN 0-634-08539-5

HAL•LEONARD® CORPORATION
7777 W. BLUEMOUND RD. P.O. BOX 13819 MILWAUKEE, WI 53213

In Australia Contact:
Hal Leonard Australia Pty. Ltd.
22 Taunton Drive P.O. Box 5130
Cheltenham East, 3192 Victoria, Australia
Email: ausadmin@halleonard.com

For all works contained herein:
Unauthorized copying, arranging, adapting, recording or public performance is an infringement of copyright.
Infringers are liable under the law.

Visit Hal Leonard Online at
www.halleonard.com

CONTENTS

Take Me Away	9
Together	13
Don't Tell Me	18
He Wasn't	25
How Does It Feel	32
My Happy Ending	39
Nobody's Home	45
Forgotten	49
Who Knows	54
Fall to Pieces	60
Freak Out	66
Slipped Away	71

TAKE ME AWAY

Words and Music by AVRIL LAVIGNE, DON GILMORE and EVAN TAUBENFELD

TOGETHER

Words and Music by AVRIL LAVIGNE
and CHANTAL KREVIAZUK

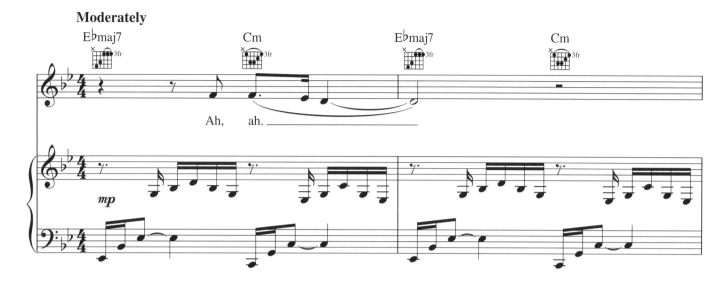

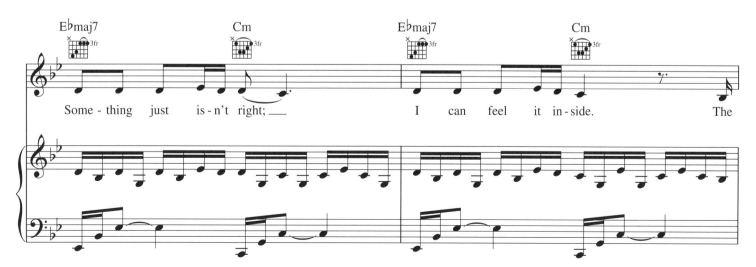

Copyright © 2004 ALMO MUSIC CORP., AVRIL LAVIGNE PUBLISHING LTD., SONY/ATV MUSIC PUBLISHING CANADA and NEVERWOULDATHOT MUSIC
All Rights for AVRIL LAVIGNE PUBLISHING LTD. Controlled and Administered by ALMO MUSIC CORP.
All Rights for SONY/ATV MUSIC PUBLISHING CANADA and NEVERWOULDATHOT MUSIC Administered by SONY/ATV MUSIC PUBLISHING, 8 Music Square West, Nashville, TN 37203
All Rights Reserved   Used by Permission

DON'T TELL ME

Words and Music by AVRIL LAVIGNE
and EVAN TAUBENFELD

HOW DOES IT FEEL

Words and Music by AVRIL LAVIGNE
and CHANTAL KREVIAZUK

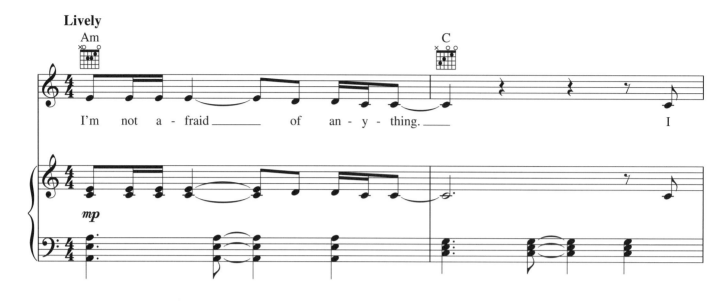

I'm not a-fraid of an-y-thing. I

just need to know that I can breathe.

I don't need much of an-y-thing. But

Copyright © 2004 ALMO MUSIC CORP., AVRIL LAVIGNE PUBLISHING LTD., SONY/ATV MUSIC PUBLISHING CANADA and NEVERWOULDATHOT MUSIC
All Rights for AVRIL LAVIGNE PUBLISHING LTD. Controlled and Administered by ALMO MUSIC CORP.
All Rights for SONY/ATV MUSIC PUBLISHING CANADA and NEVERWOULDATHOT MUSIC Administered by SONY/ATV MUSIC PUBLISHING, 8 Music Square West, Nashville, TN 37203
All Rights Reserved   Used by Permission

MY HAPPY ENDING

Words and Music by AVRIL LAVIGNE
and BUTCH WALKER

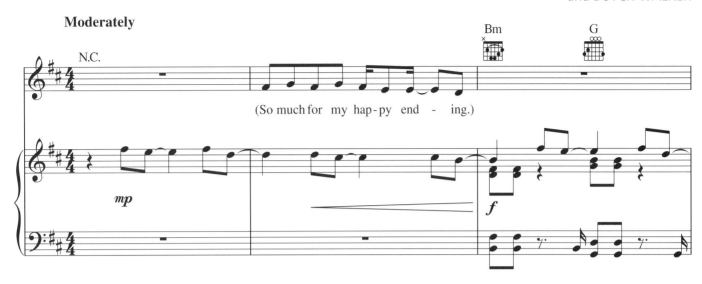
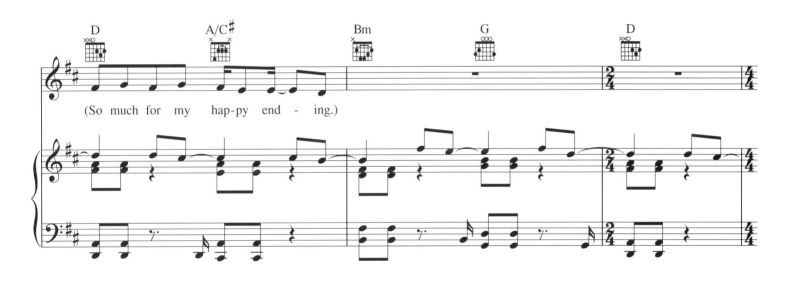
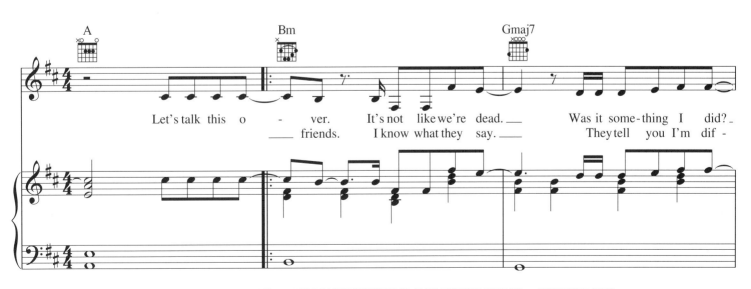

Copyright © 2004 ALMO MUSIC CORP., AVRIL LAVIGNE PUBLISHING LTD., EMI Blackwood Music Inc. and Sonotrock Music
All Rights for AVRIL LAVIGNE PUBLISHING LTD. Controlled and Administered by ALMO MUSIC CORP.
All Rights for SONOTROCK MUSIC Controlled and Administered by EMI BLACKWOOD MUSIC INC.
All Rights Reserved Used by Permission

NOBODY'S HOME

45

Words and Music by AVRIL LAVIGNE,
DON GILMORE and BEN MOODY

Copyright © 2004 ALMO MUSIC CORP., AVRIL LAVIGNE PUBLISHING LTD., LA QUINTA SONGS, DWIGHT FRYE MUSIC INC. and SMELLSLIKEMETAL PUBLISHING
All Rights for AVRIL LAVIGNE PUBLISHING LTD. and LA QUINTA SONGS Controlled and Administered by ALMO MUSIC CORP.
All Rights Reserved   Used by Permission

FALL TO PIECES

Words and Music by AVRIL LAVIGNE
and RAINE MAIDA

Copyright © 2004 ALMO MUSIC CORP., AVRIL LAVIGNE PUBLISHING LTD., SONY/ATV MUSIC PUBLISHING CANADA and UNDER ZENITH MUSIC, INC.
All Rights for AVRIL LAVIGNE PUBLISHING LTD. Controlled and Administered by ALMO MUSIC CORP.
All Rights for SONY/ATV MUSIC PUBLISHING CANADA and UNDER ZENITH MUSIC, INC. Administered by SONY/ATV MUSIC PUBLISHING, 8 Music Square West, Nashville, TN 37203
All Rights Reserved   Used by Permission

FREAK OUT

Words and Music by AVRIL LAVIGNE,
EVAN TAUBENFELD and MATTHEW BRANN

Copyright © 2004 ALMO MUSIC CORP., AVRIL LAVIGNE PUBLISHING LTD., EMI APRIL MUSIC INC., EVAN TAUBENFELD MUSIC and MATTHEW BRANN
All Rights for AVRIL LAVIGNE PUBLISHING LTD. Controlled and Administered by ALMO MUSIC CORP.
All Rights for EVAN TAUBENFELD MUSIC Controlled and Administered by EMI APRIL MUSIC INC.
All Rights Reserved   Used by Permission